DressUp Chappell

Dress Up Chappell

ILLUSTRATED BY JULIA MURRAY

A CHAPPELL ROAN
PAPER DOLL BOOK
FEATURING HER
MOST ICONIC LOOKS

AN UNOFFICIAL AND
UNAUTHORIZED PAPER DOLL BOOK

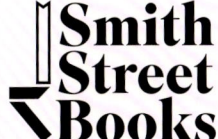

Smith
Street
Books

Instructions

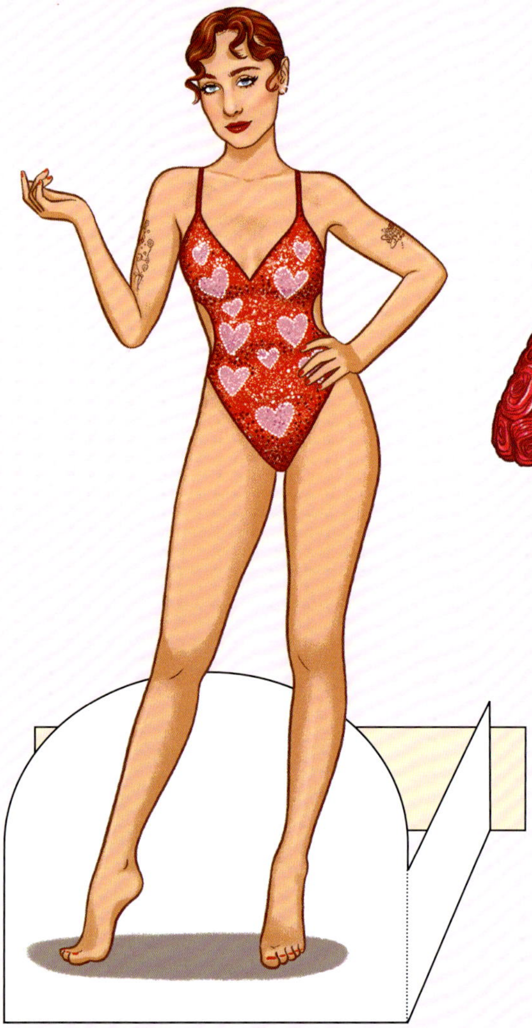

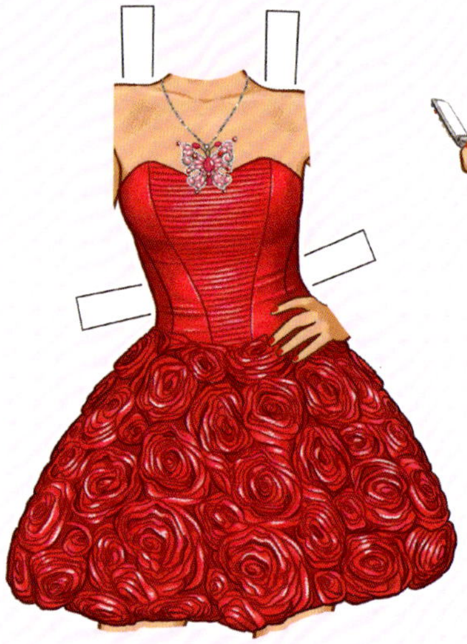

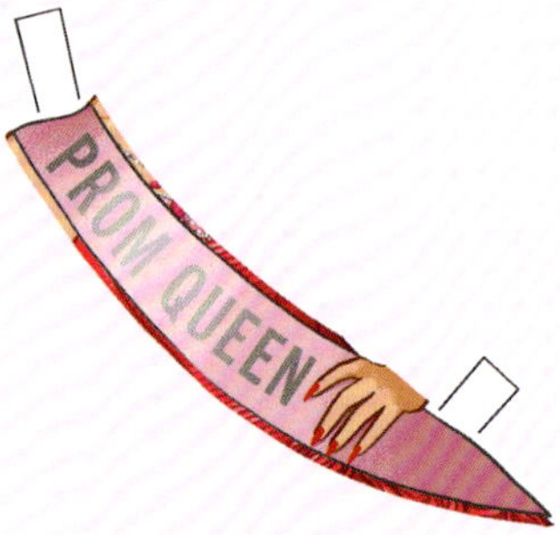

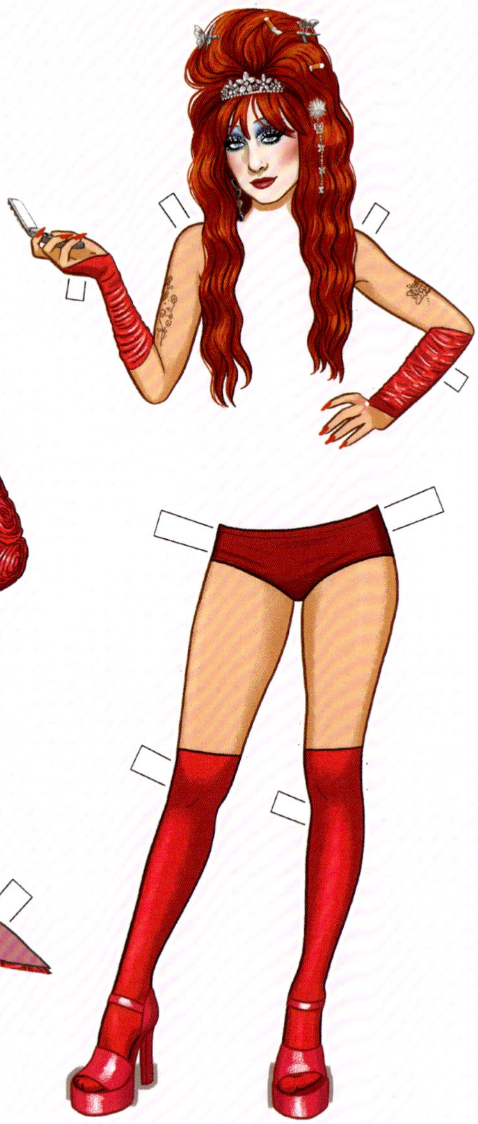

TO USE, CAREFULLY PRESS OUT THE DOLL AND CROSS-PIECE AND ASSEMBLE THE STAND AS SHOWN BELOW.

PRESS OUT THE OUTFITS AND GET DRESSING. DRESS CHAPPELL IN HER ICONIC LOOKS OR TRY MIXING AND MATCHING.

SLOT CROSS-PIECE INTO THE FLAPS.

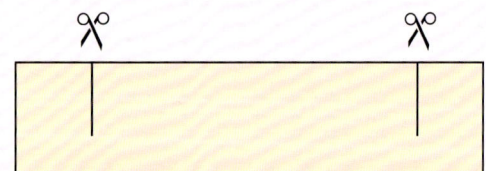

USE SCISSORS TO SNIP THE CROSS-PIECE AND STAND.

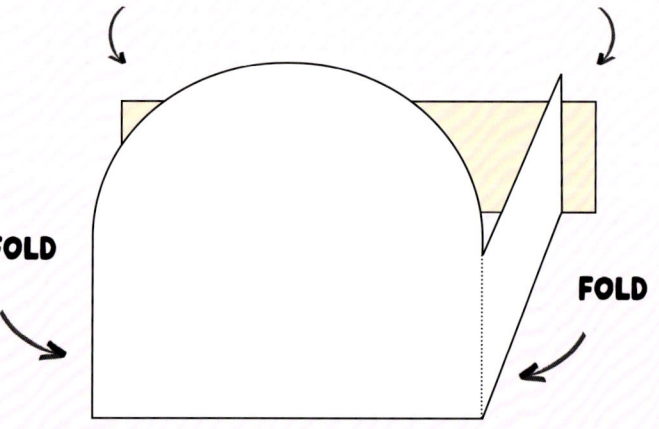

FOLD

FOLD

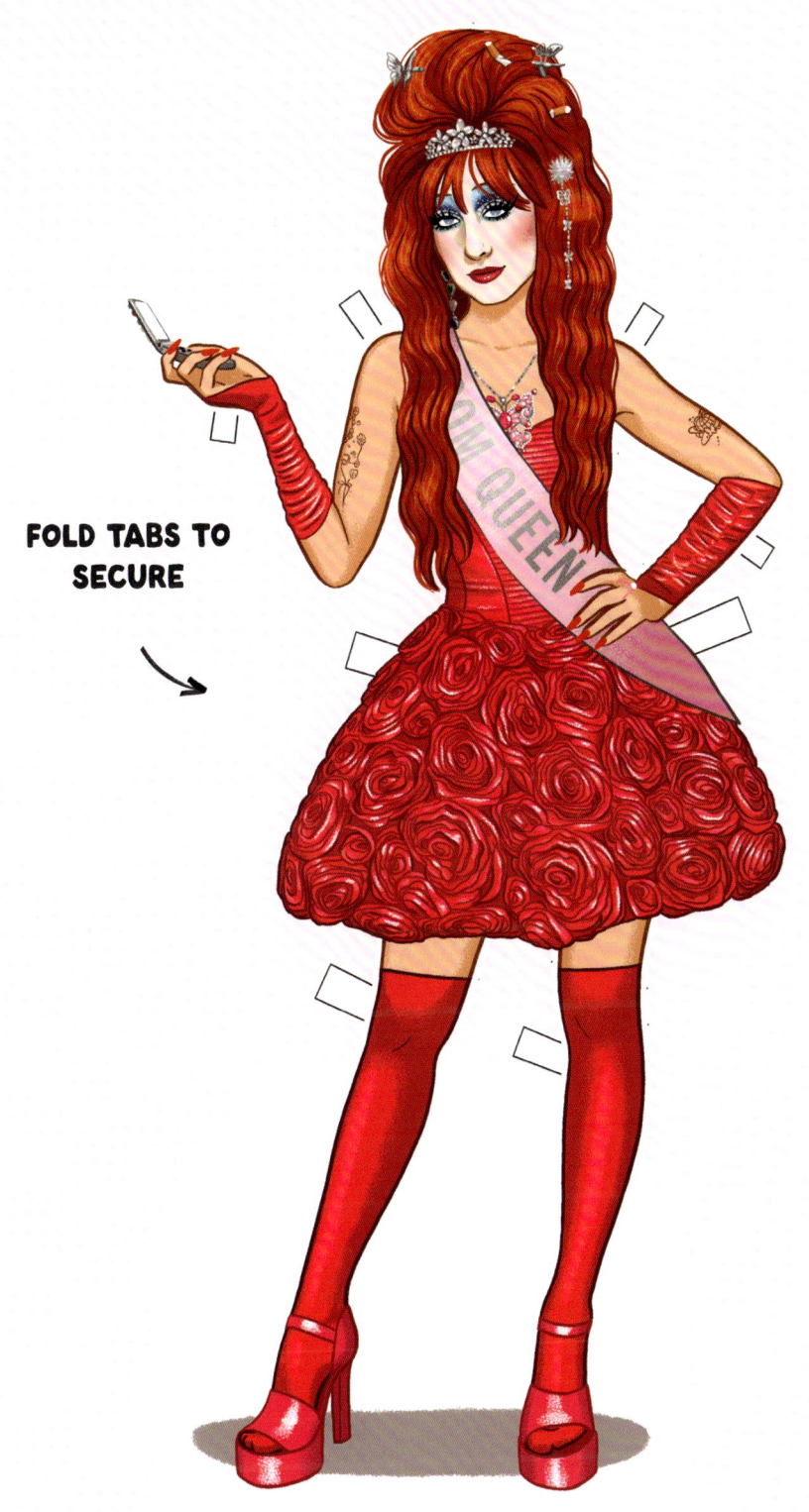

FOLD TABS TO
SECURE

My Kink Is Karma

music video, 2023

Red lace bra with tassels and fishnet stockings, rhinestone tassel choker, vintage cheetah jacket, and Pleaser Moon-708HRS platform heels.

Costume design, hair, and makeup by Chappell Roan

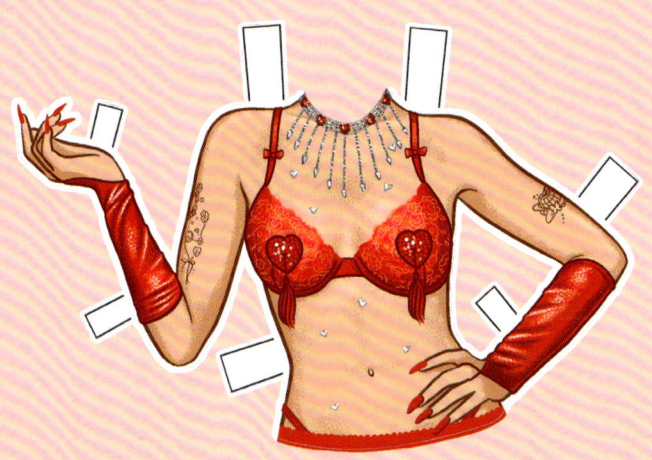

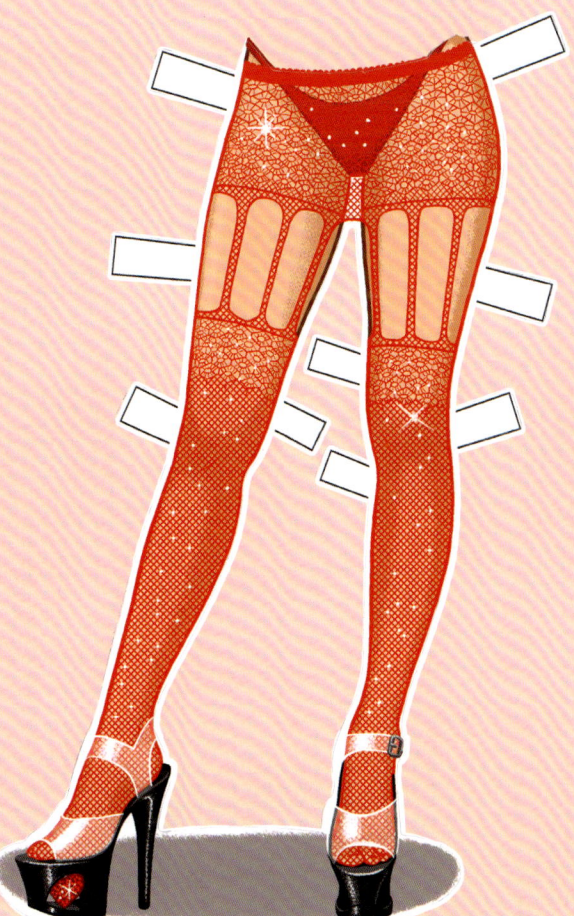

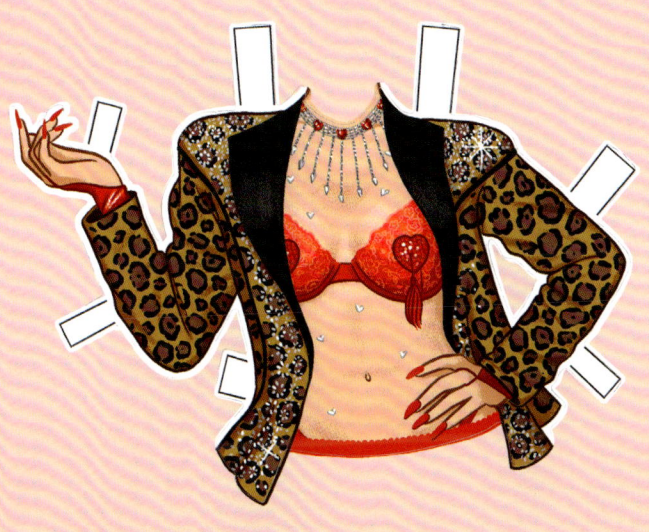

Hot to Go!

music video, 2023

Palace Costumes vintage marching band unitard and jacket with gold gogo boots.

Styled by Genesis Webb
Hair and makeup by Chappell Roan

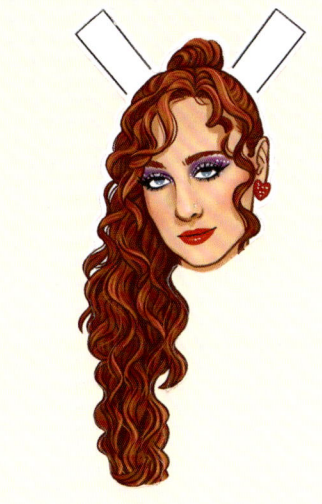

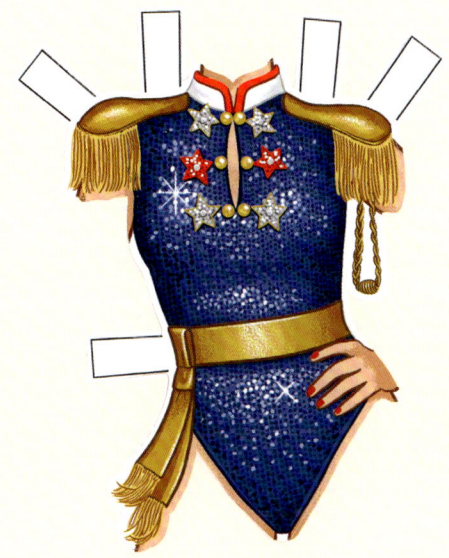

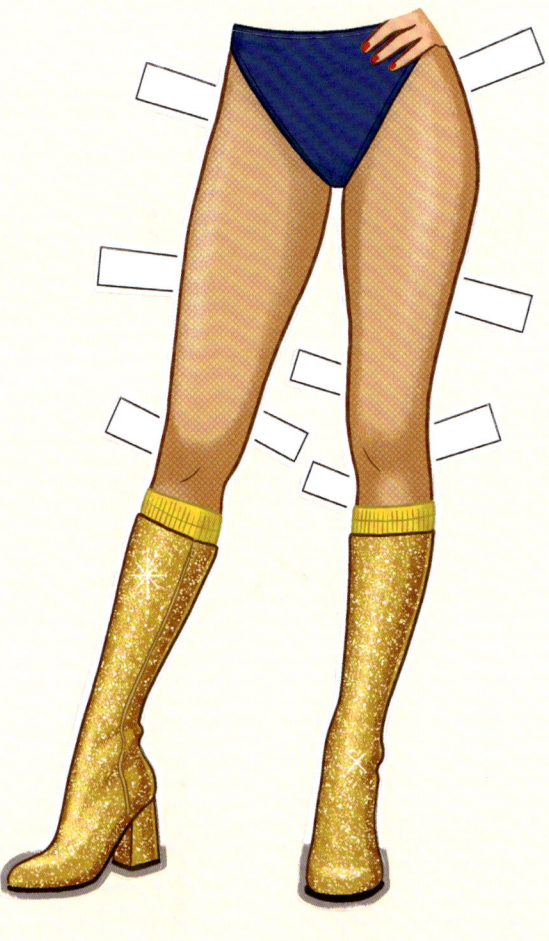

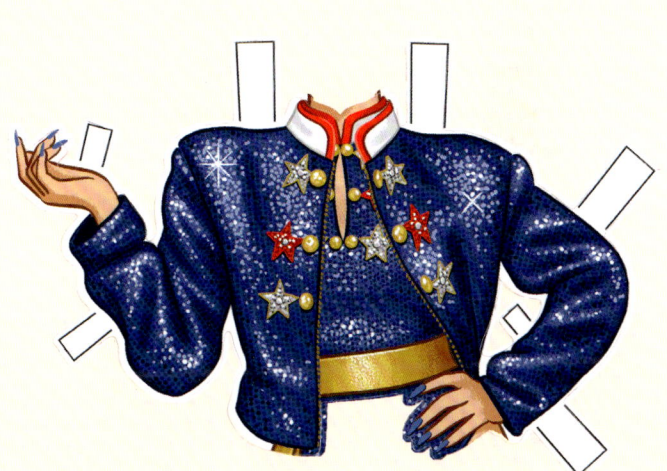

NPR
Tiny Desk Concert

2024

Vintage Betsey Johnson Rose Topiary
dress and butterfly necklace, with pink
tights, pink gloves and patent pink
platform shoes.

Styled by Genesis Webb
Hair (wig) by Dom Forletta
Makeup by Sterling Tull

PROM QUEEN

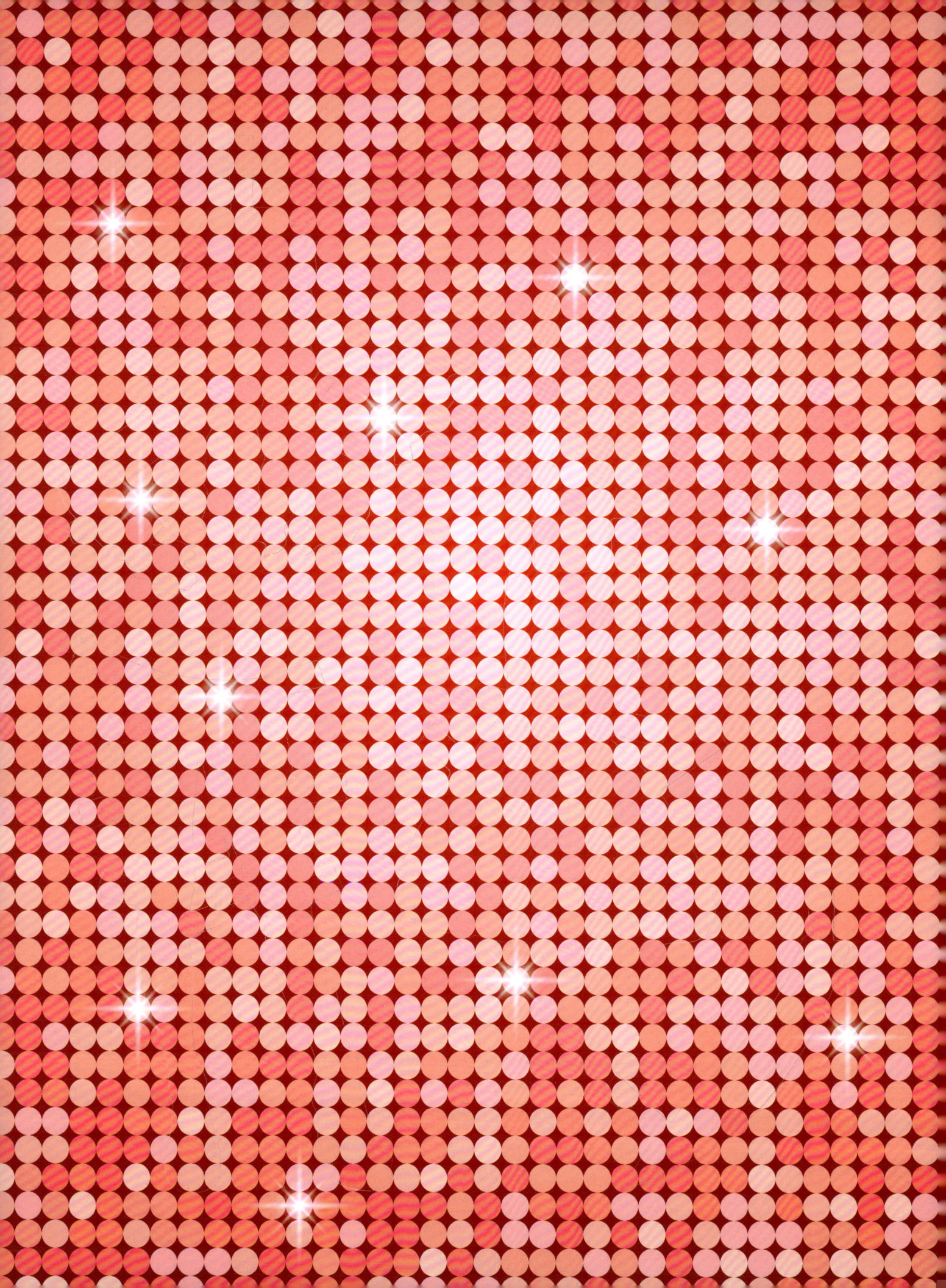

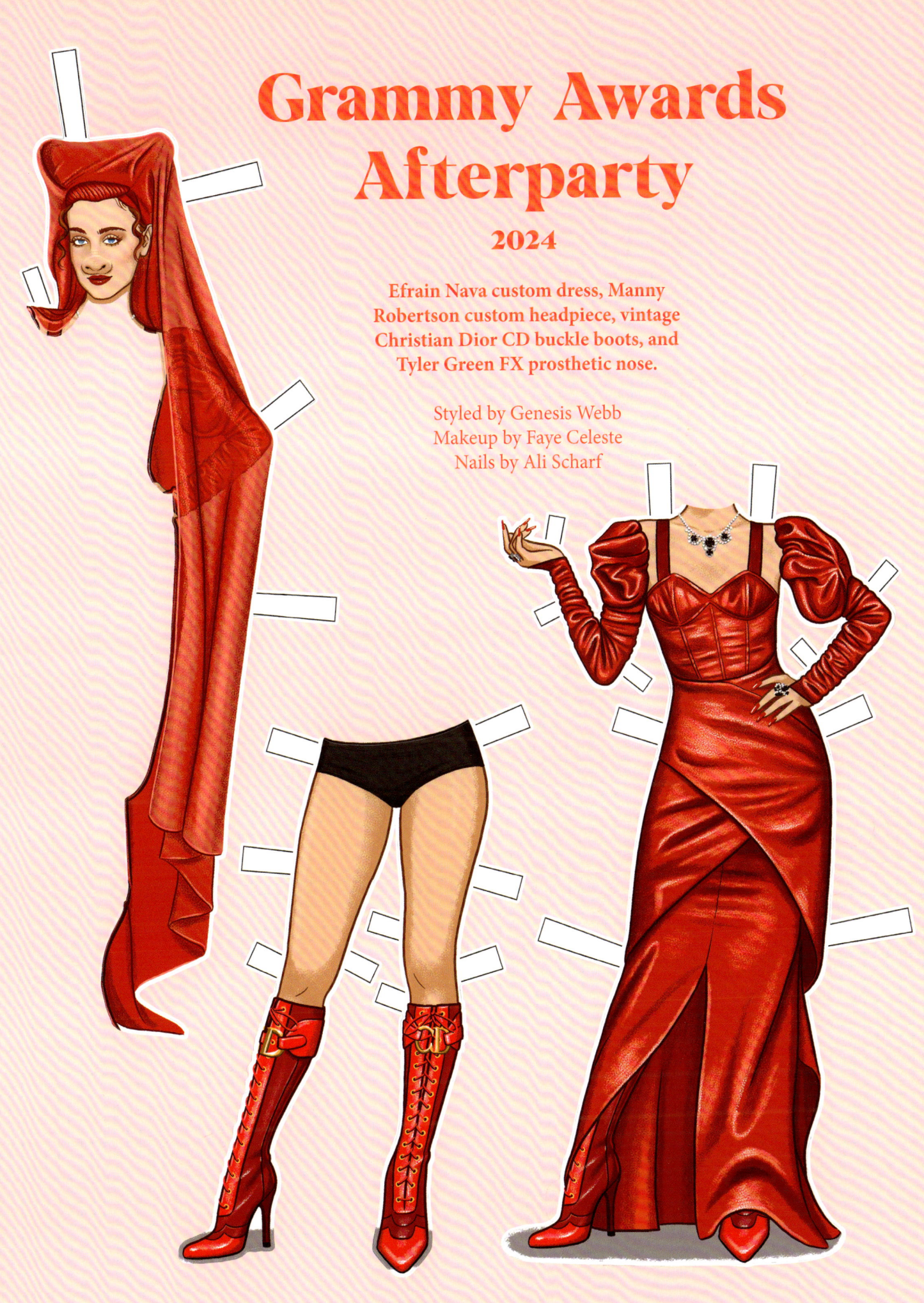

Grammy Awards Afterparty

2024

Efrain Nava custom dress, Manny Robertson custom headpiece, vintage Christian Dior CD buckle boots, and Tyler Green FX prosthetic nose.

Styled by Genesis Webb
Makeup by Faye Celeste
Nails by Ali Scharf

Governors Ball

2024

Monique Fei custom dress,
Daniel Bosco custom crown
and torch, and Journee
Collection knee-high boots.

Styled by Genesis Webb
Hair by Dom Forletta
Makeup by Andrew Dahling
Nails by Samantha Diaz

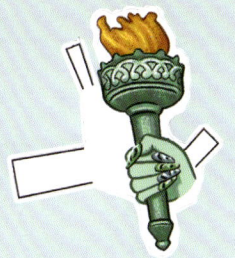

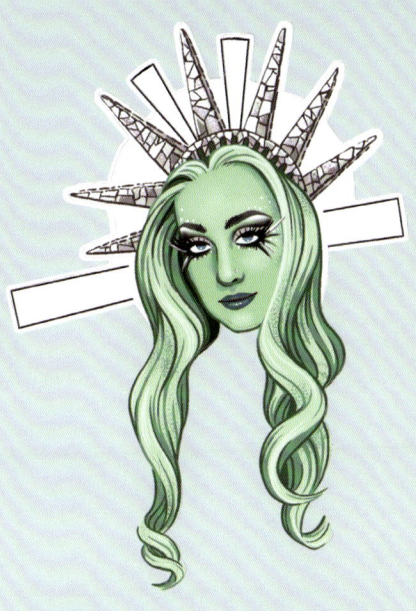

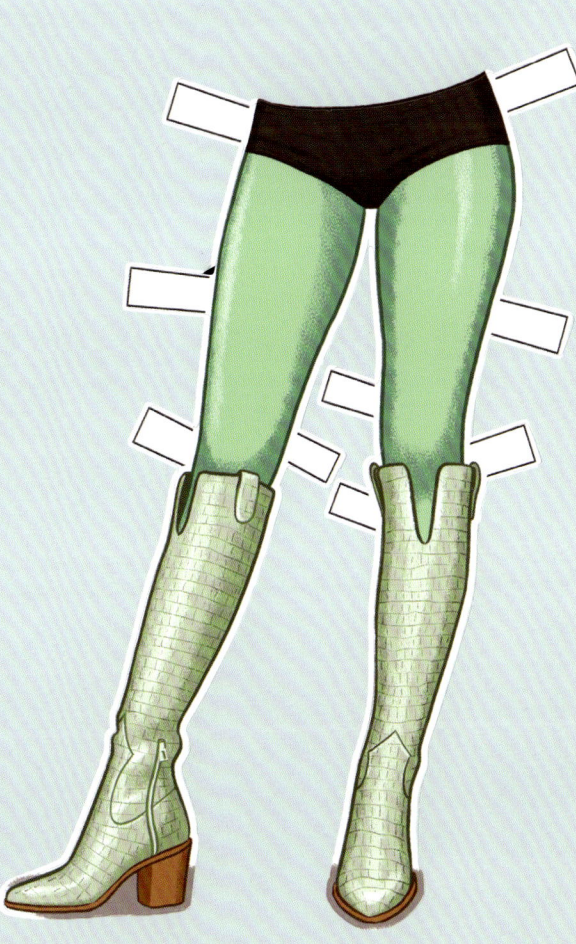

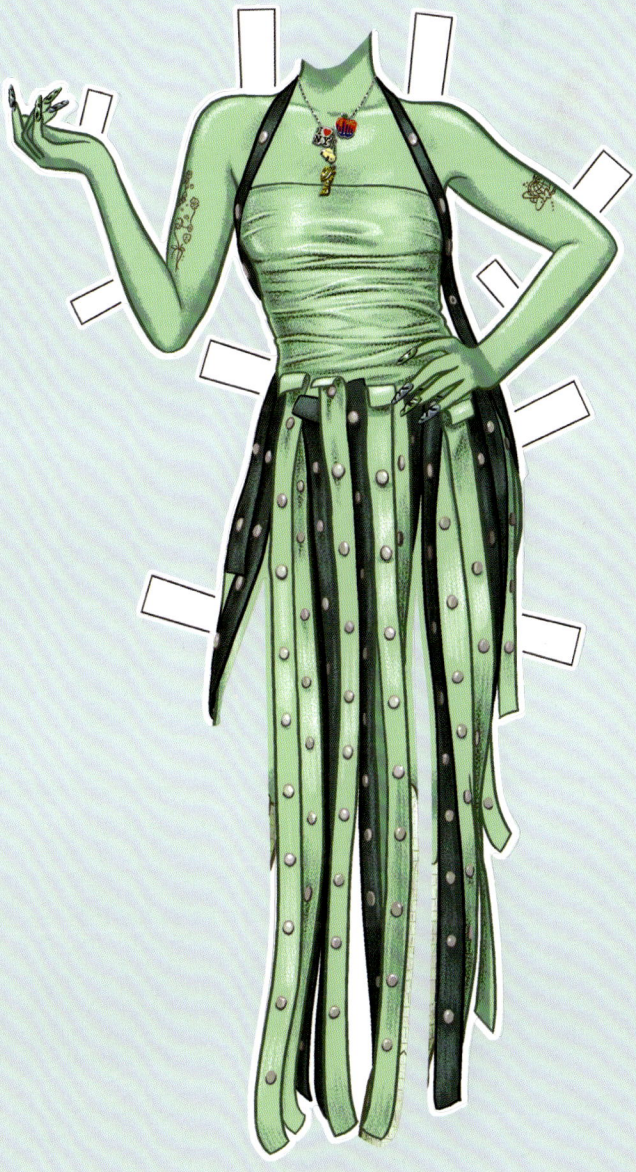

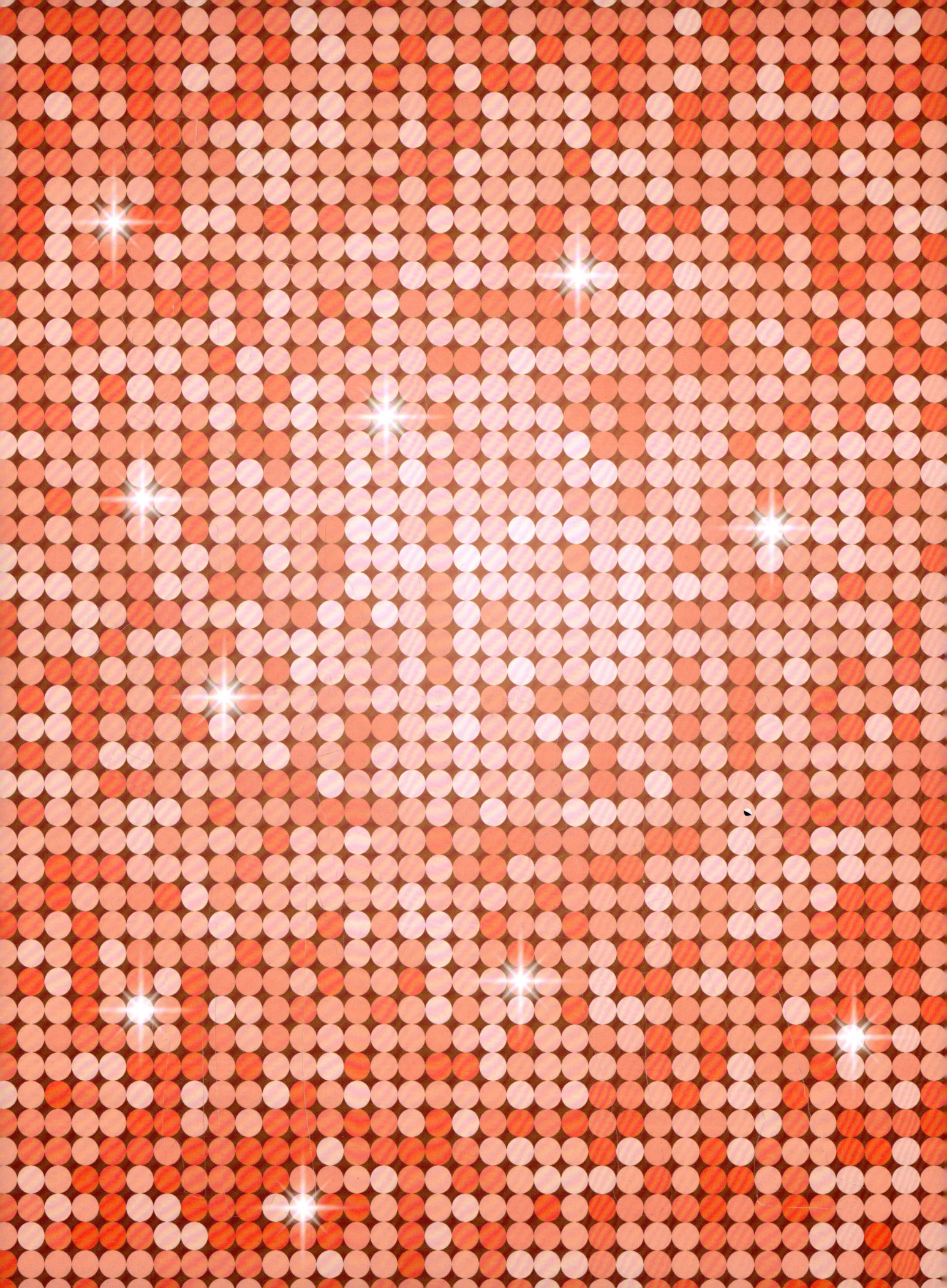

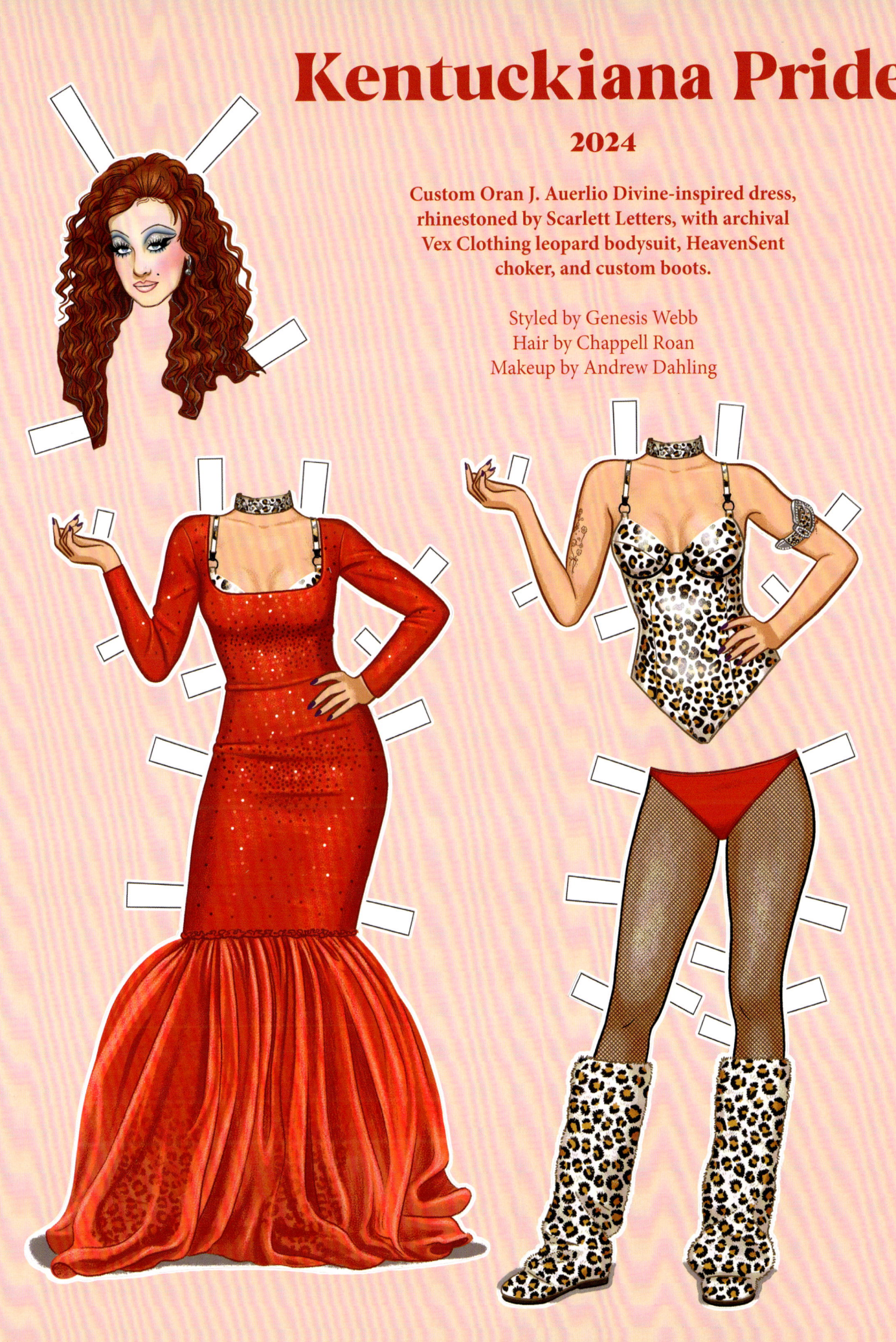

Kentuckiana Pride

2024

Custom Oran J. Auerlio Divine-inspired dress, rhinestoned by Scarlett Letters, with archival Vex Clothing leopard bodysuit, HeavenSent choker, and custom boots.

Styled by Genesis Webb
Hair by Chappell Roan
Makeup by Andrew Dahling

The Tonight Show
Starring Jimmy Fallon
2024

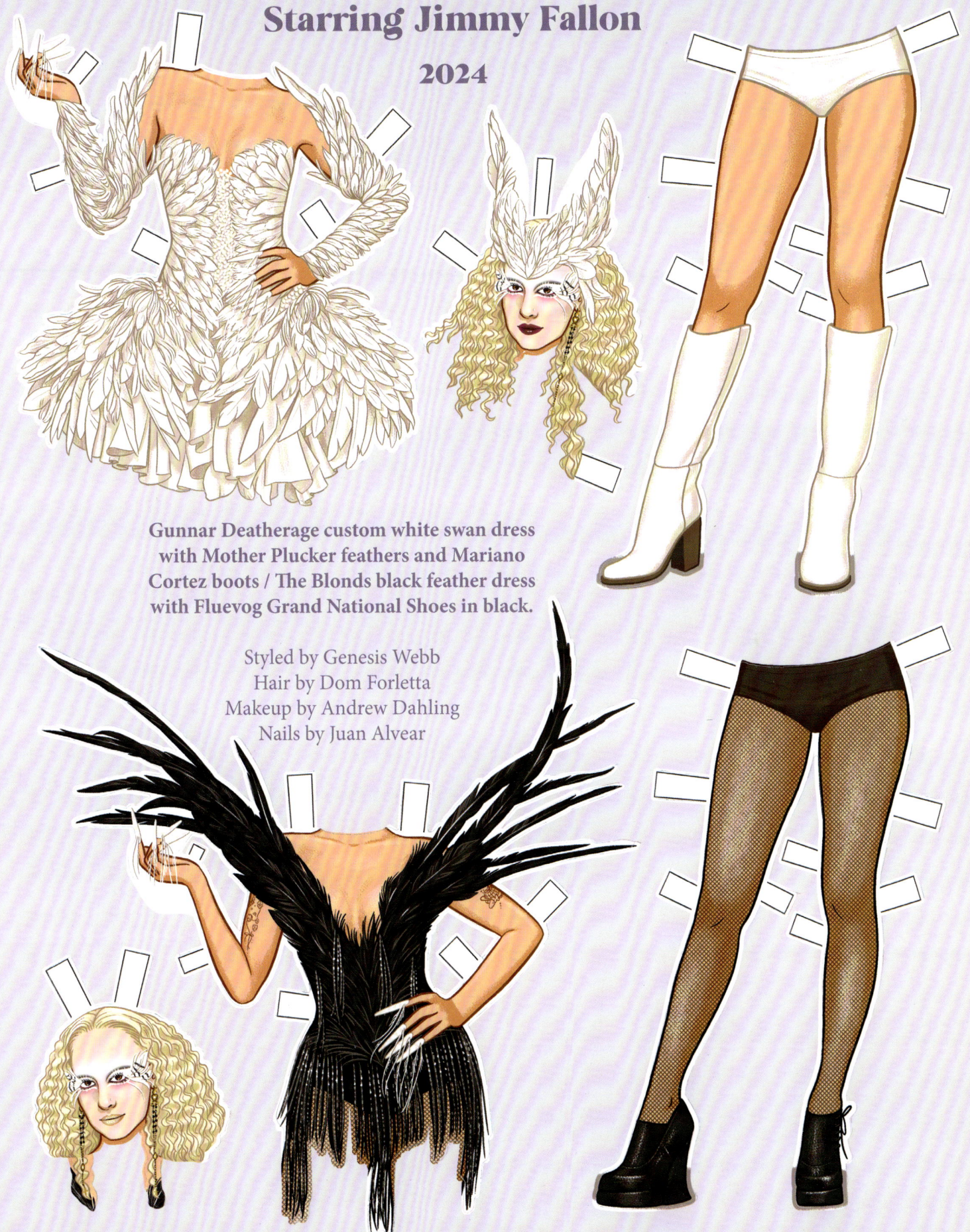

Gunnar Deatherage custom white swan dress with Mother Plucker feathers and Mariano Cortez boots / The Blonds black feather dress with Fluevog Grand National Shoes in black.

Styled by Genesis Webb
Hair by Dom Forletta
Makeup by Andrew Dahling
Nails by Juan Alvear

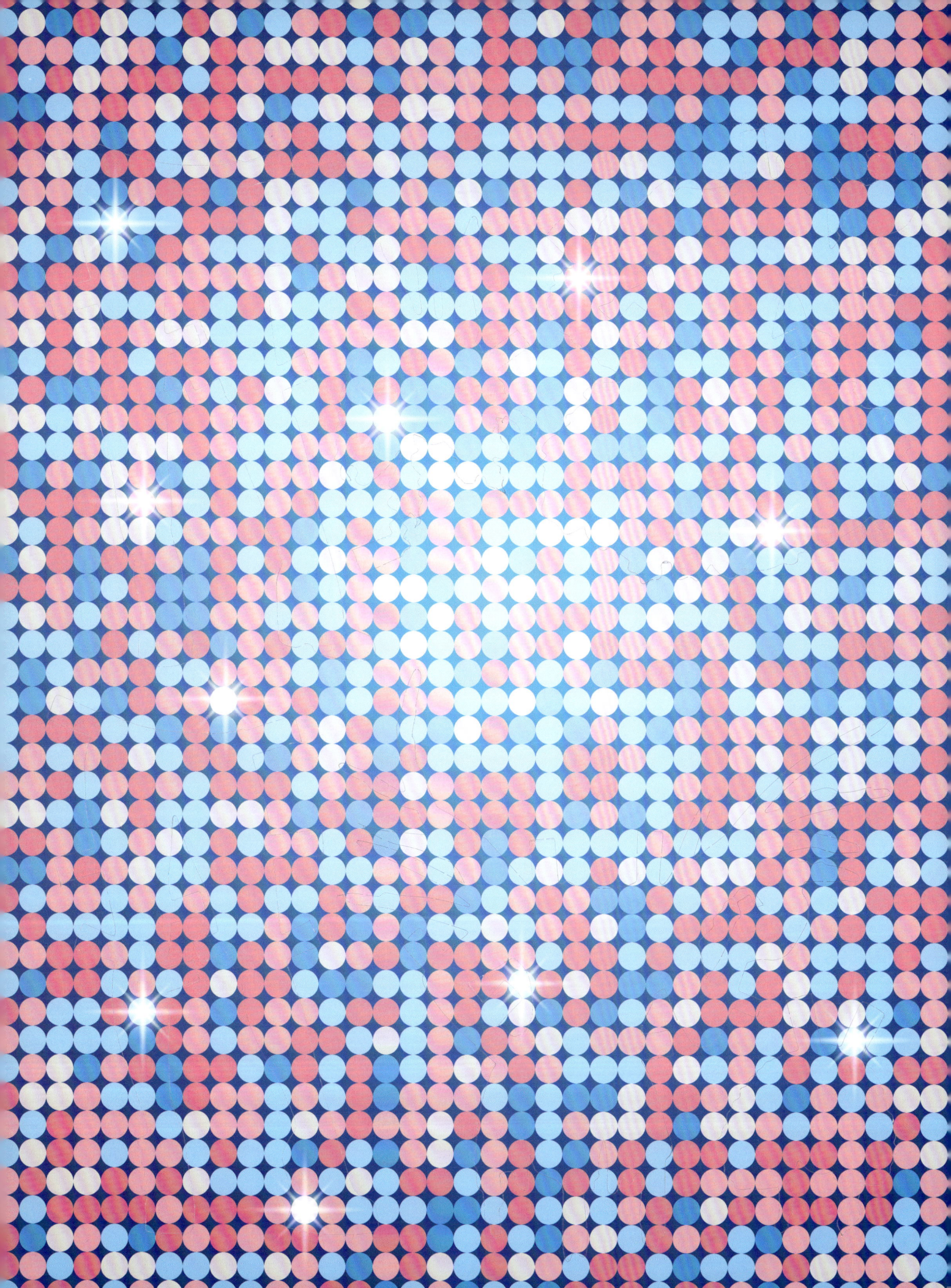

Lollapalooza

2024

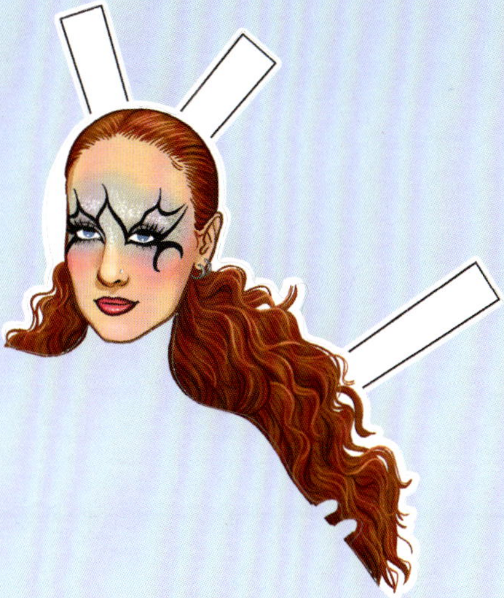

Busted Brand bodysuit, with Zana
Bayne mask, wrist cuffs, and belt,
and Adidas Japan VH sneaker boots.

Styled by Genesis Webb
Hair by Dom Forletta
Makeup by Ali Scharf

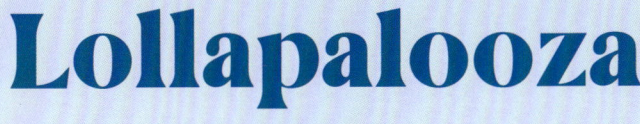

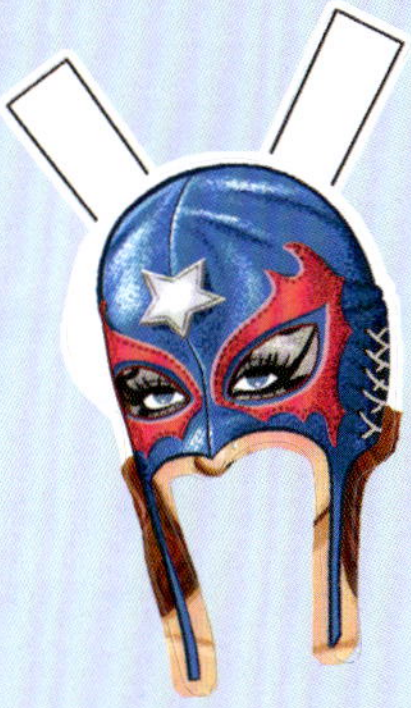

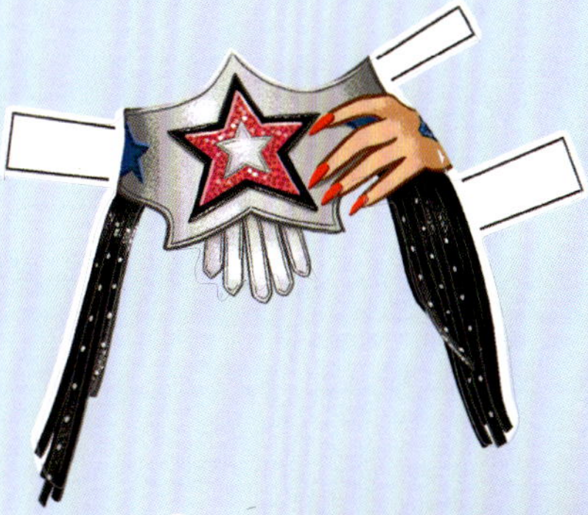

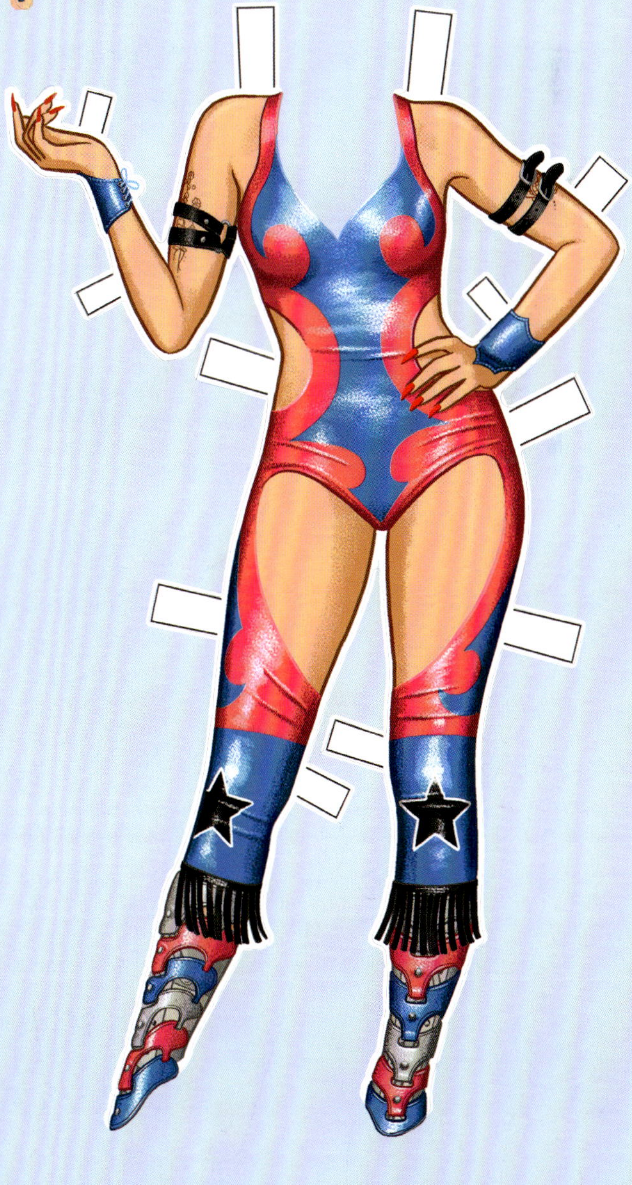

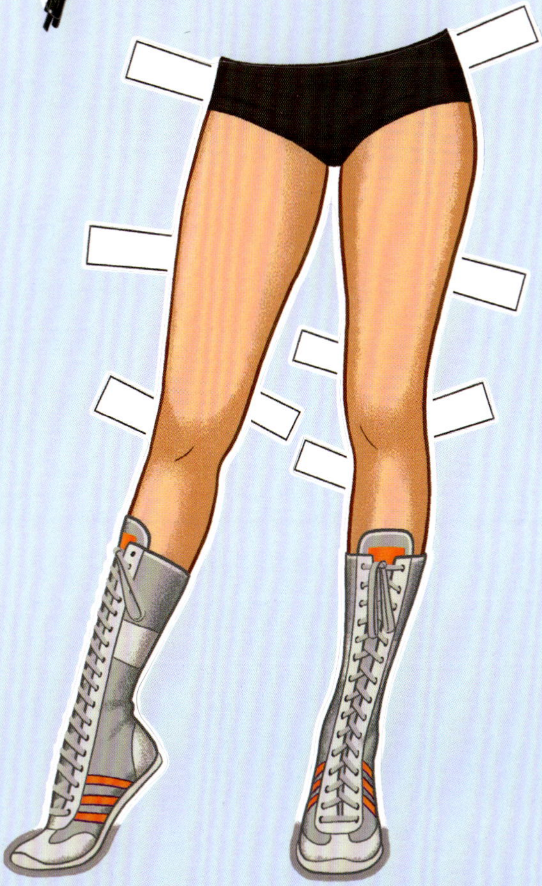

VMAs

performing "Good Luck, Babe!", 2024

Zana Bayne armor and Dr. Martens
Anistone Hi boots, with custom bow
and arrow.

Styled by Genesis Webb
Hair by Dom Forletta
Makeup by Andrew Dahling
Nails by Juan Alvear

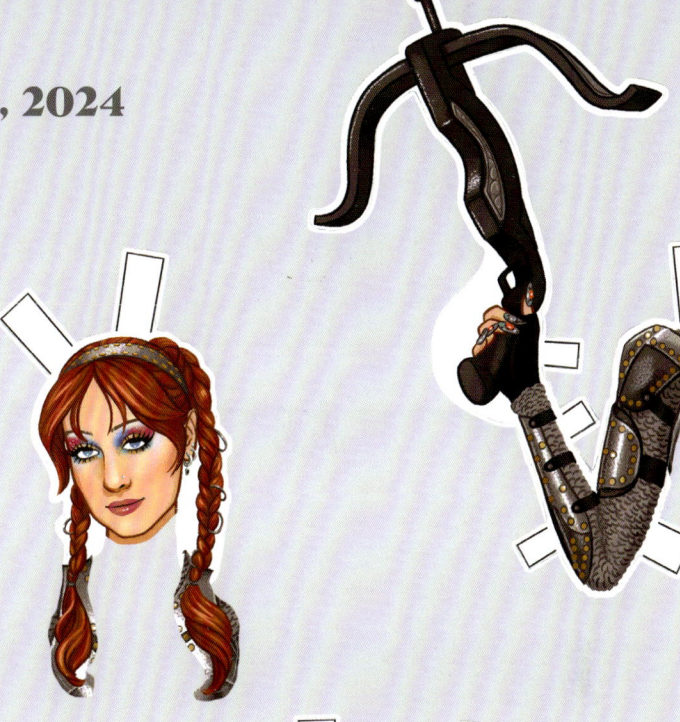

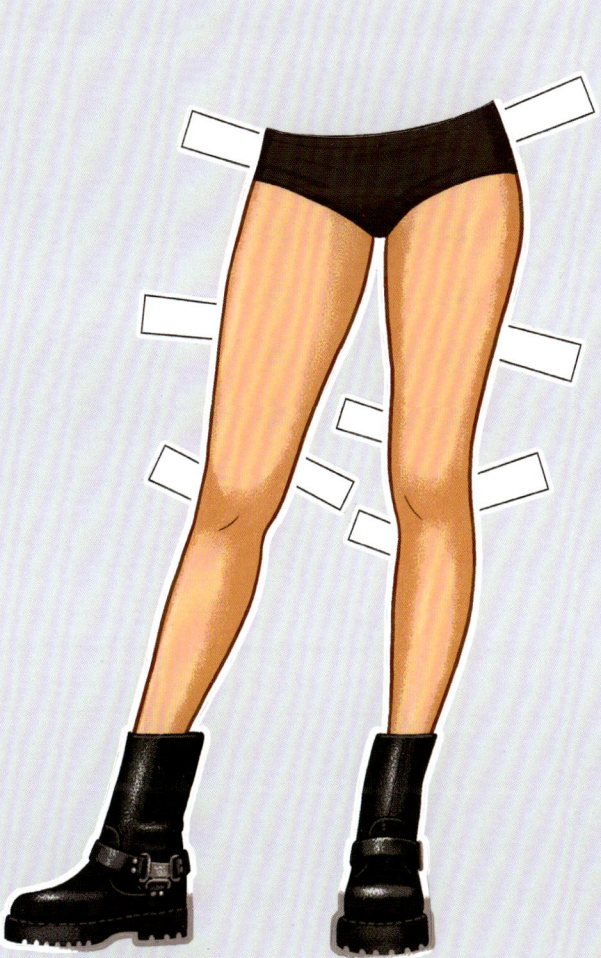

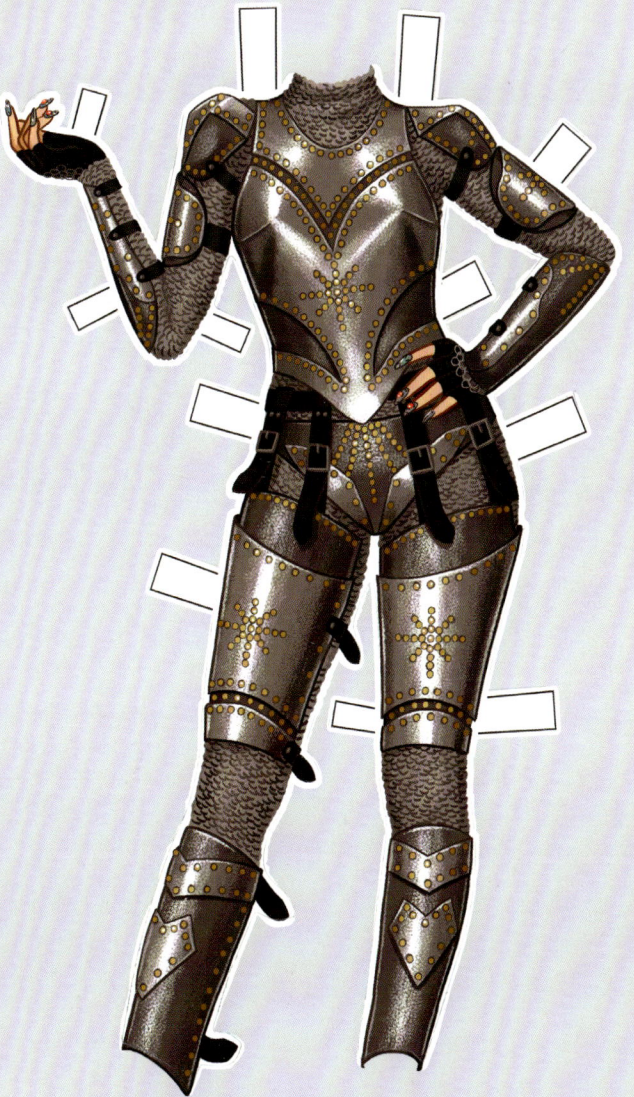

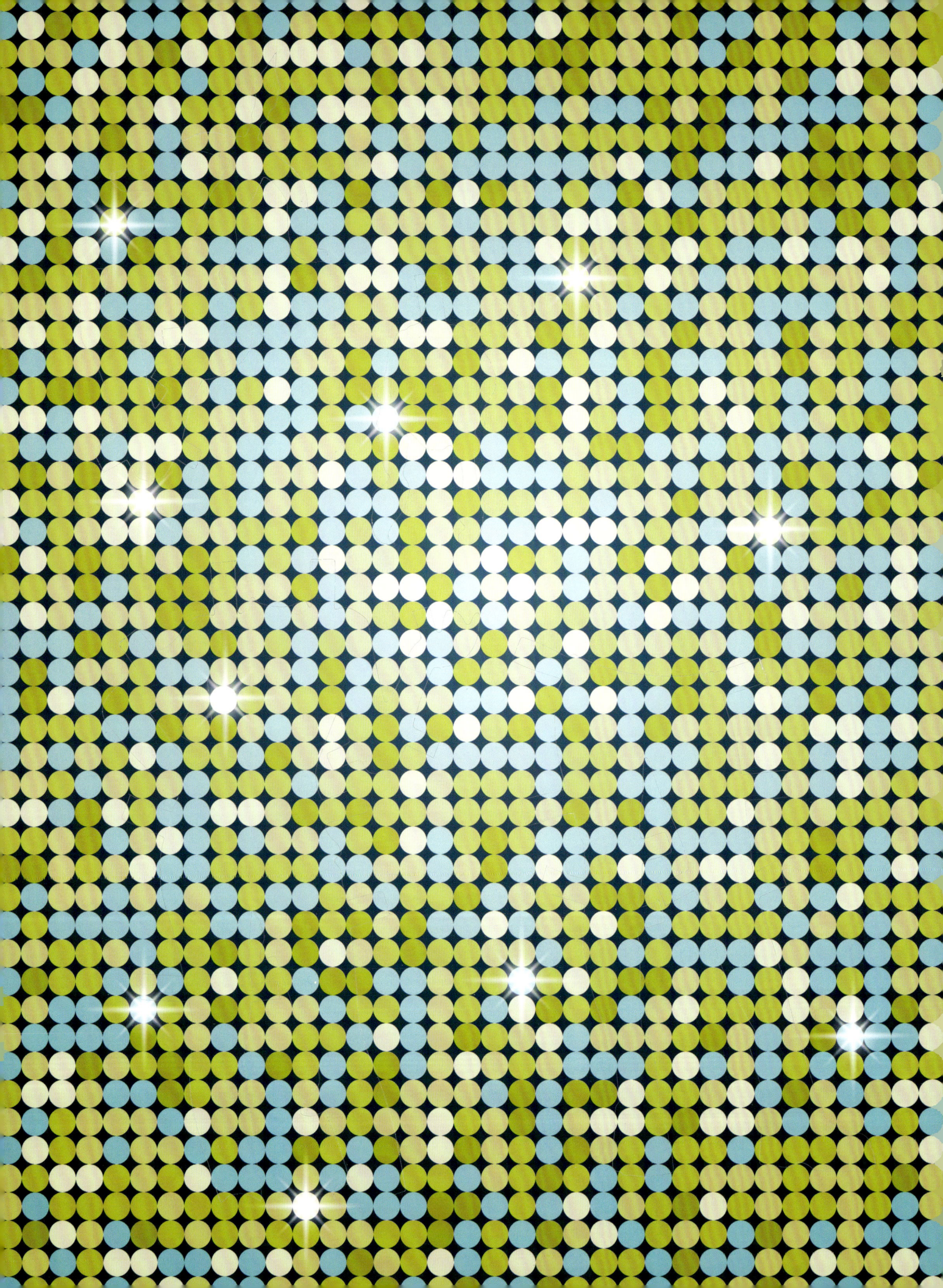

SNL

2025

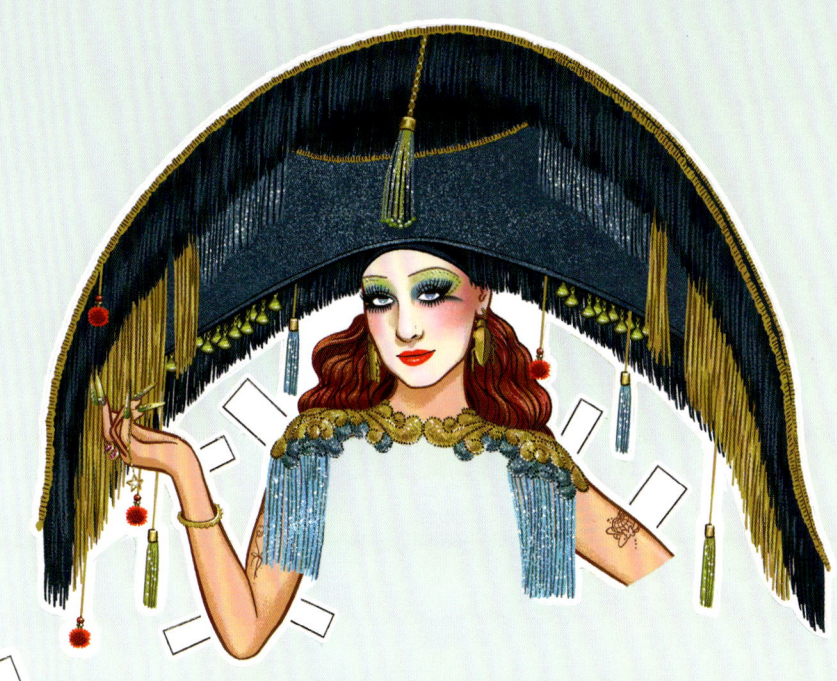

Gunnar Deatherage and Katie Maimi
winged bodysuit, Christopher Minafo
headpiece, custom tights, and Thom
Browne shoes.

Styled by Genesis Webb
Hair by Dom Forletta
Makeup by Andrew Dahling
Nails by Juan Alvear

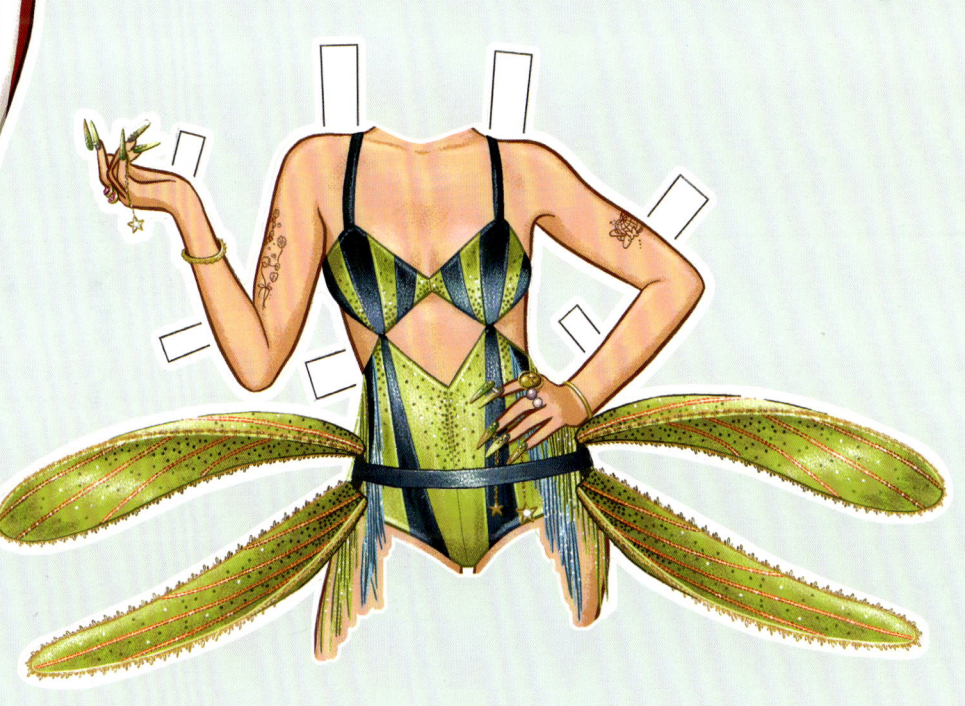

Grammy Awards

red carpet, 2025

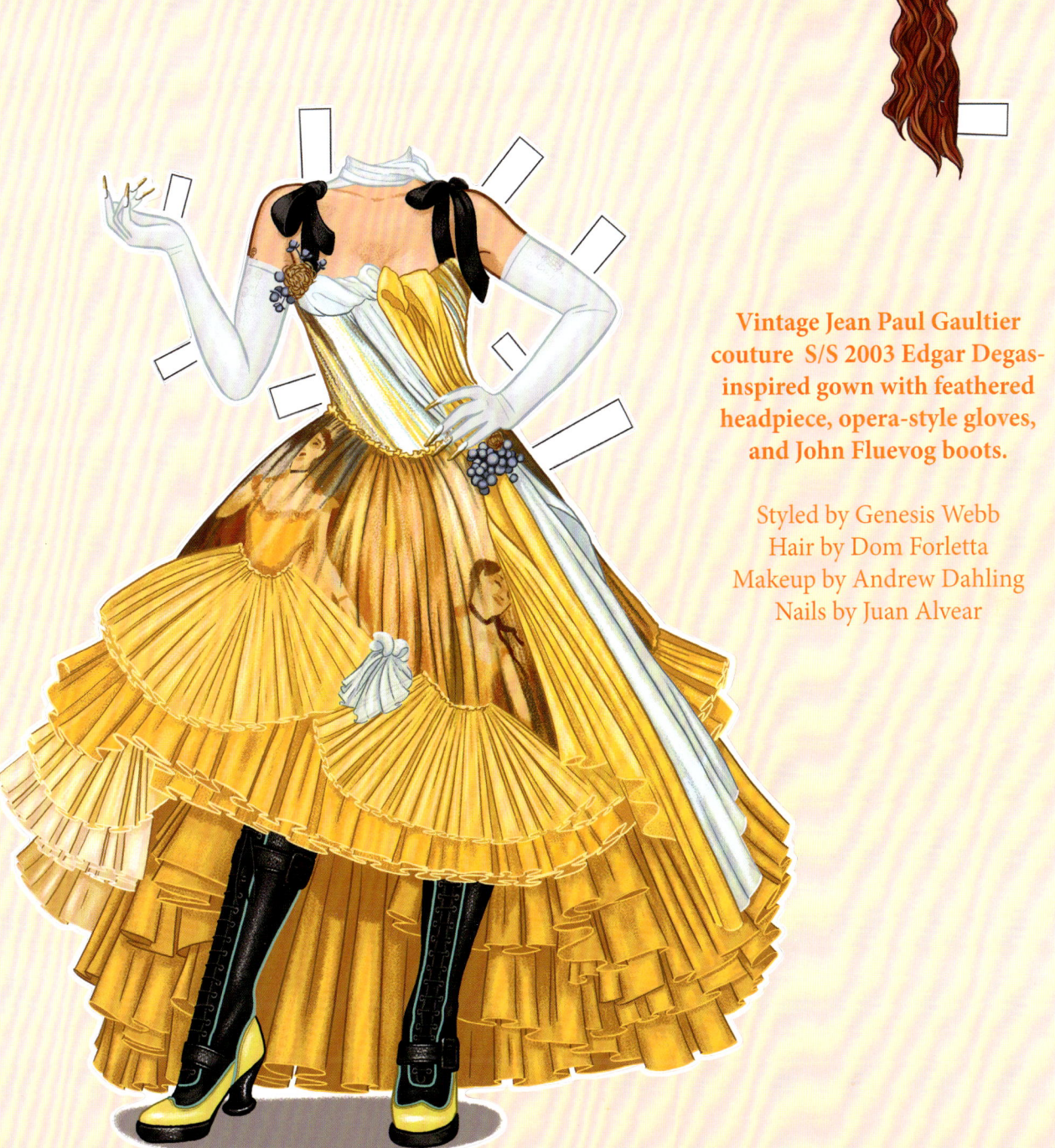

Vintage Jean Paul Gaultier couture S/S 2003 Edgar Degas-inspired gown with feathered headpiece, opera-style gloves, and John Fluevog boots.

Styled by Genesis Webb
Hair by Dom Forletta
Makeup by Andrew Dahling
Nails by Juan Alvear

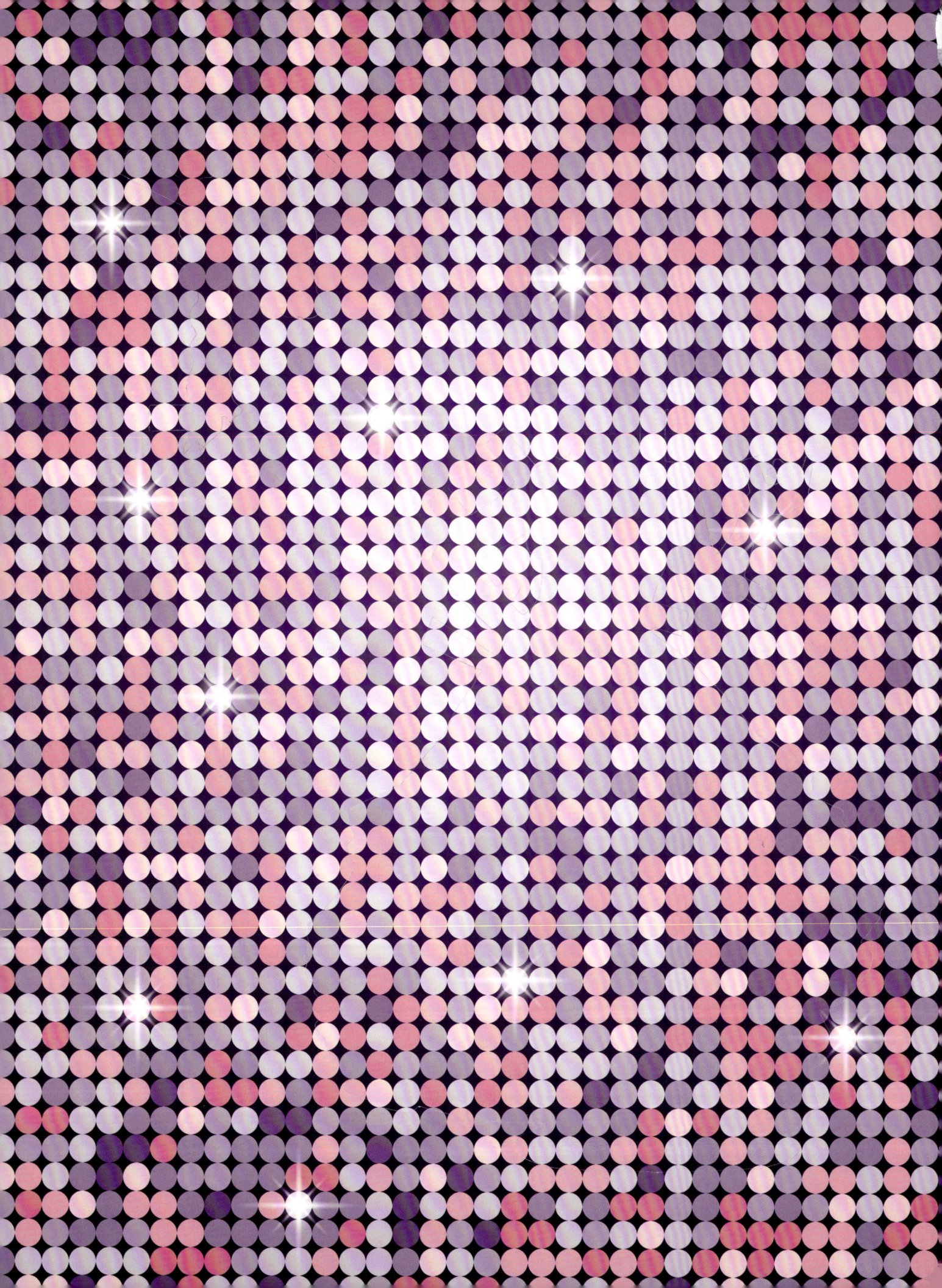

Grammy Awards

performing "Pink Pony Club," 2025

Custom Zana Bayne leather leotard and boots with Gunnar Deatherage hat.

Styled by Genesis Webb
Hair by Dom Forletta
Makeup by Andrew Dahling
Nails by Juan Alvear

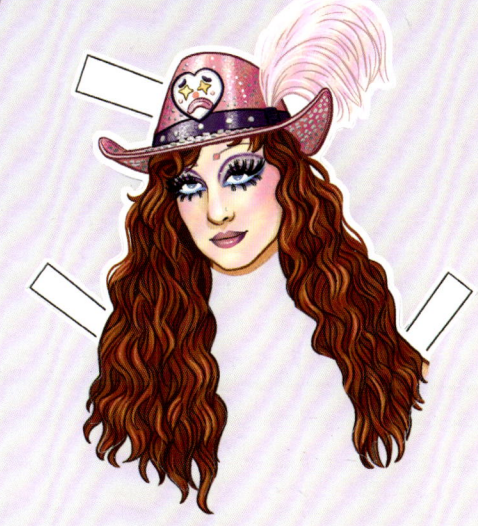

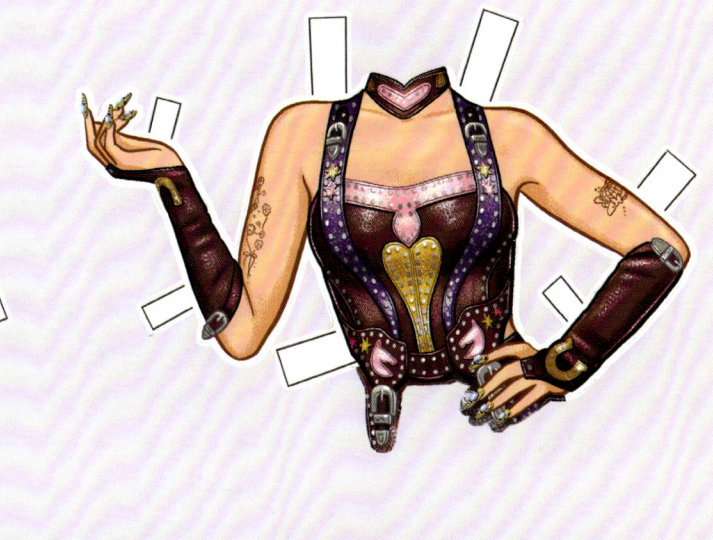

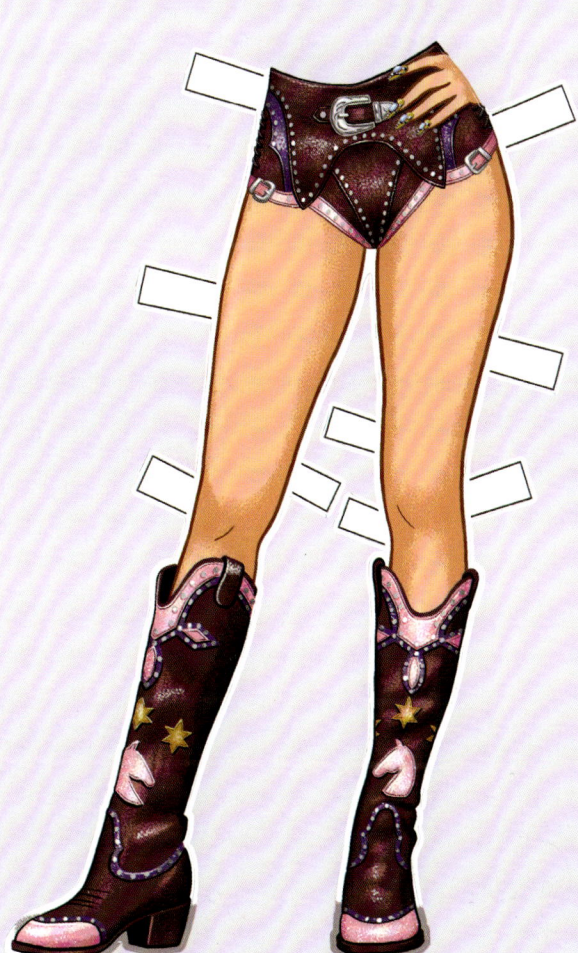

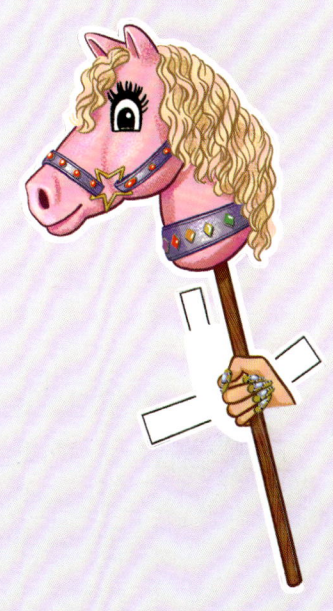

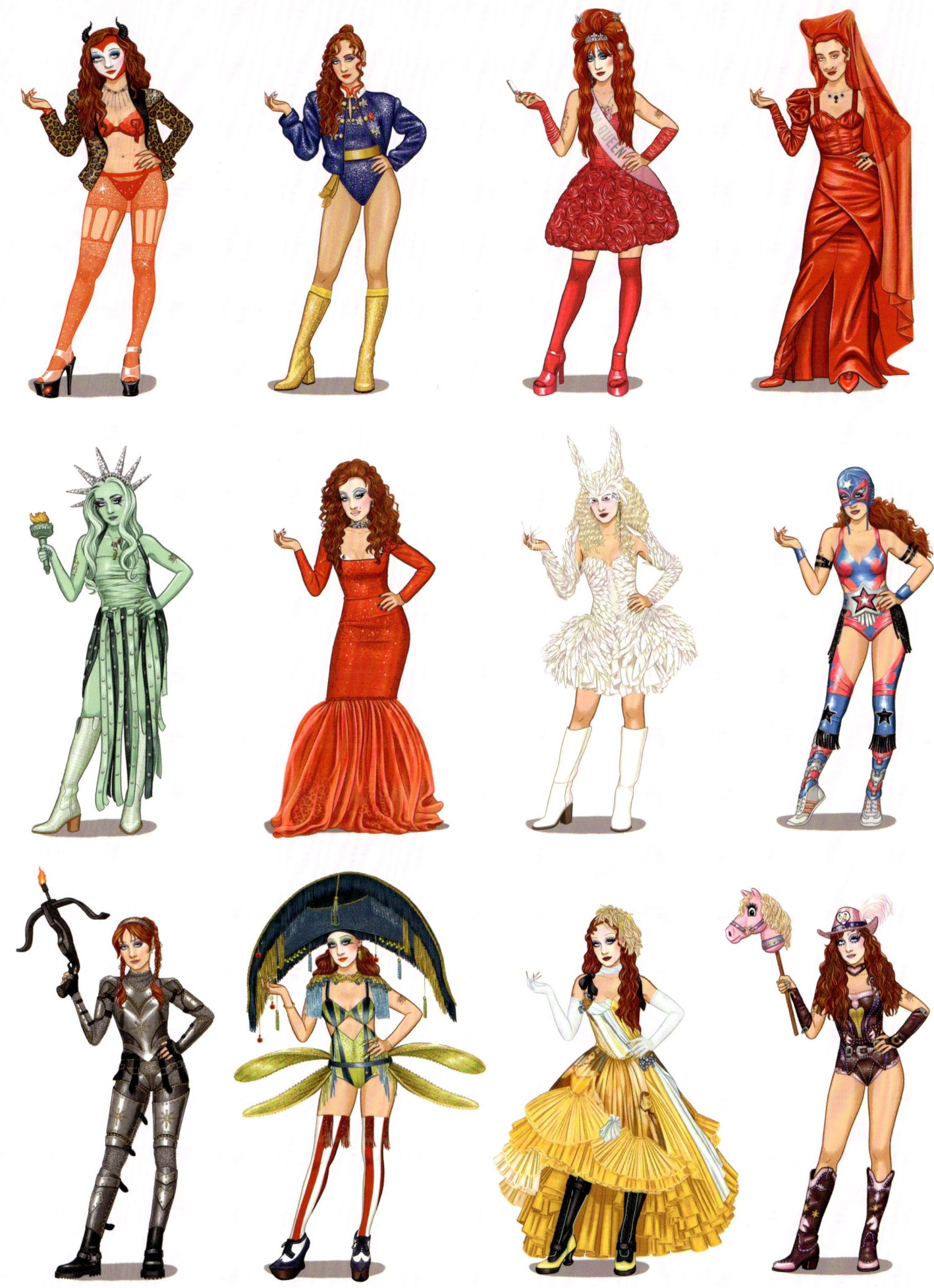

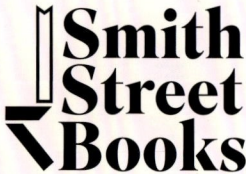

Published in 2025 by Smith Street Books
Naarm (Melbourne) | Australia
smithstreetbooks.com

Distributed outside of ANZ, North & Latin America by
Thames & Hudson Ltd., 6–24 Britannia Street, London, WC1X 9JD
thamesandhudson.com

EU Authorised Representative: Interart S.A.R.L.
19 rue Charles Auray, 93500 Pantin, Paris, France
productsafety@thameshudson.co.uk; www.interart.fr

ISBN: 978-1-9232-3968-5
Urban Outfitters exclusive edition ISBN: 978-1-9232-3996-8

Smith Street Books respectfully acknowledges the Wurundjeri People of the Kulin Nation,
who are the Traditional Owners of the land on which we work, and we pay our respects
to their Elders past and present.

Publisher: Hannah Koelmeyer
Editor: Lucy Grant
Illustrator: Julia Murray
Series design: Alissa Dinallo
Patterns via Adobe Stock, customised by Milla Freeman
Production manager: Aisling Coughlan
Proofreader: Ariana Klepac
Prepress: Megan Ellis

Printed & bound in China by C&C Offset Printing Co., Ltd.

Book 426
10 9 8 7 6 5 4 3 2 1

Please note: This title is not affiliated with or endorsed in any way by Chappell Roan.
We are just big fans.